Tornadoes

By Myrl Shireman
Illustrated By John Kaufmann

COPYRIGHT © 2006 Mark Twain Media, Inc.

ISBN 1-58037-371-2

Printing No. D04126

Mark Twain Media, Inc., Publishers
Distributed by Carson-Dellosa Publishing Company, Inc.

Level 5: Book 4

Tornadoes vs Straight-line Winds

Tornadoes are very destructive storms that occur in many parts of the world. Although they may happen throughout the year, the spring and summer seasons bring increased concern. Typically, they occur in the afternoon when storms with thunder, lightning, and heavy rain are most likely. They are very common in the Great Plains and Midwest. The term "Tornado Alley" is used to refer to those parts of the Great Plains and Midwest where sightings are frequent. But this storm strikes in many places, including the mountains at higher elevations. Anytime there is a storm with thunder, lightning, and heavy rain, a tornado may develop.

A thunderstorm with a rope tornado

Great Plains Midwest
Tornado Alley

The high, towering clouds of a thunderstorm have an anvil-shaped top.

Almost everyone has looked up into the sky where there was a high, towering cloud. Many times, the cloud has an anvil-shaped top. These high, towering clouds are a warning that a severe storm is possible, with lightning, thunder, heavy rain, and strong winds. These strong winds can be very destructive and are called **straight-line winds**. Tornadoes, however, are not straight-line winds. Tornado winds **spiral**, or spin. They spiral at a high rate of speed in and around the center, or eye, of a low-pressure area.

Thunderstorms

When is a thunderstorm most likely? The storm is
a result of a large mass of warm, humid air rising rapidly
up from the earth's surface. In spring and summer, there
are long, warm days, and the air near the earth's surface
becomes very warm. Such an air mass is often loaded with
water vapor, which is water in gas form. The air mass
becomes unstable and is likely to rise.

Warm Air

Clouds form when warm air rises and cools. The water vapor in the air condenses into droplets to form a cloud.

Rising higher and higher, the air mass becomes cooler and cooler. If it cools enough, the water vapor in the air changes to small droplets of liquid water, and clouds form. When the water vapor changes to liquid water, it is called **condensation**. If the air mass rises high enough, the clouds become taller and taller and become anvil shaped.

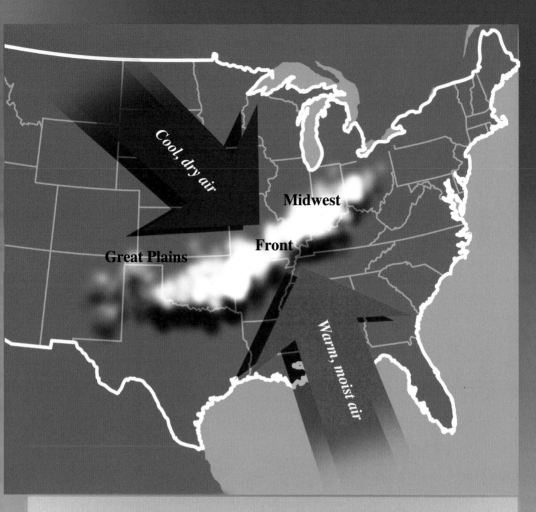

Cool, dry air

Midwest

Great Plains

Front

Warm, moist air

In the United States, thunderstorms often develop when a large, warm, moist air mass from over the Gulf of Mexico moves north. The air mass moves north into the Great Plains and Midwest. There the warm, moist air mass from the Gulf often meets a cooler, drier air mass from the north. When these two very unlike air masses meet, they do not mix. The warm, moist air from over the Gulf is lighter, so it rises over the cooler, heavier, and drier air mass. A boundary forms between the warmer and cooler air. Along this boundary, a **front** is formed. It is along this front that severe storms and tornadoes are possible.

Classifying Tornadoes

When tornadoes form, the winds begin to move in toward a low-pressure area. Around the low-pressure area, the winds are spinning around the center, or **eye**, of the low-pressure area. Then the winds move upward. The air spins counterclockwise around the eye. As the winds spin around the center, or eye, the winds may reach speeds of 100 to 200 miles per hour. Such high winds can be very destructive. However, the area of destruction may be a mile or less in width. A scale is used to rank tornado wind speed. The scale ranks are F0, F1, F2, F3, F4, or F5. F0 and F1 are very weak. The most violent is the F5 where winds may be greater than 200 miles per hour.

The winds on the earth's surface move counterclockwise in toward the base of a tornado that reaches into the atmosphere.

Hail

How does hail form? A thunderstorm forms because an unstable air mass begins to rise from the earth's surface. As the air mass rises, it cools, and condensation occurs. When this happens, clouds form. Some clouds rise higher and higher, to heights of 25,000 feet or more.

Strong Updraft

Droplets of water are blown up and down inside the cloud. The droplets freeze, thaw, and refreeze. This forms hail.

Inside the cloud at this high altitude, there are ascending air currents, or **updrafts**, and descending air currents, or **downdrafts**. The updrafts carry droplets of water high into the cloud where the droplets freeze. A downdraft then carries the frozen droplets down to a lower level where the droplets thaw. Up and down, the droplets of water travel. During this time, the droplets of water are freezing, thawing, and then refreezing. They become larger and larger. When they become heavy enough, they drop to the ground as hail.

Hail can be very damaging to cars and other property.

When warm, moist air rises above cool, dry air, it forms a front. Thunderstorms may form along this front.

Weather Forecasts

Forecasts that predict possible tornadoes are often made when storm fronts form between warm and cool air masses. Rapidly upward-flowing air is found along the storm front boundary where warm, moist air and cool, drier air meet. When the two air masses meet, the warm, moist air is forced up over the drier, heavier, cooler air. When the warm, moist air is forced up rapidly, it cools, and thunderstorms are likely. In these storms, the clouds often begin to spin. Any cloud that is spinning should be of concern to those in a storm path.

Today, weather forecasts alert people when there is danger of a severe storm. Thunderstorms and tornadoes are very dangerous. Therefore, forecasts are made to alert the public. The forecast may be a **watch**. A watch means that conditions exist for a tornado. The forecast may be a **warning**. A warning means that a tornado has been sighted.

Tornado winds spiral in a counterclockwise direction around the eye of a low-pressure area.

Types of Tornadoes

In a storm, the high, towering clouds may spin. To be a tornado, the spinning cloud must extend from the cloud to the ground. The spinning cloud may be rope-shaped or wedge-shaped. A rope tornado has a funnel shape. The rope is narrow, tube-like, and extends from the cloud to the ground. The rope is very visible. A wedge tornado does not look like a rope. It is much wider. However, both have counterclockwise winds moving in and up around a low-pressure area that is the center, or eye.

Rope Tornado

Wedge Tornado

The lifting force of a tornado may be great enough to lift very heavy objects, such as roofs and cars. The rising air around the eye may carry lighter objects high into the atmosphere. Small objects can be carried miles before they are dropped back to earth. In 2003, a tornado struck Canton, Missouri. Pictures and other objects were carried from Canton across the Mississippi River. Many objects were later found across the river many miles away.

Tornadoes may last only a few seconds, but many do last much longer. They often touch down at one place and then bounce back above the earth's surface, touching down again some miles away. The tornado's path is often much less than a mile in width. However, within the path, there may be great damage.

If a tornado occurs, go to the lowest level of the building. Get under a table or something that will protect you from falling objects.

Tornado Safety

How does one keep safe during a tornado? It is likely you have been told that opening the windows of a house will protect you. Opening the windows of any building will not make you safer. A building may be a safe place to be if the building is well built. If a building has a basement, go there. Get under a table or something that will protect you from falling objects.

During a tornado, do not take shelter under structures like bridges because of the possibility of flooding.

Beware of Flooding

If you are in a car, try to drive away from the path of the tornado. You are directly in its path if the tornado is neither on your right nor your left. If you are caught outside, do not get under structures like bridges. A bridge does protect you from flying objects, but there is always the possibility of flooding. If you are outside and cannot get to a safe building, then a low spot where you can lie down will offer some safety.